SHOPLIFTING AND THEFT ADDICTION

Participant Workbook

A Court-Approved Guide to Understanding, Overcoming, and
Managing Shoplifting and Theft Addictions

Dr. Arleen A. Fuller, Ph.D.

Table of Contents

INTRODUCTION

Welcome to Shoplifting and Theft Addiction Treatment. This group is not designed to attack you. It is designed to help you. Our goal is to deliver information that will help you prevent future episodes of theft and shoplifting.

Treatment Objectives

- ✓ Understand why you shoplift and steal.
- ✓ Prevent, reduce, and eliminate shoplifting and theft behavior.
- ✓ Help you manage and control your responses to anger and depression.
- ✓ Assist in changing your perceptions, values, thought management, and conditioning.
- ✓ Help improve your self-esteem and personal/professional development.
- ✓ Promote self-awareness, preventative strategies, and social skills.

Shoplifting and Theft

Shoplifting is the crime of taking goods from a store without payment or intent to pay. Theft is a taking of another person's property without that person's permission or consent with the intent to deprive the rightful owner of it.

Why do you think people shoplift or steal from others?

_____

_____

_____

_____

Write down the emotions/feelings that you feel before and after you commit an act of theft. Fill in the columns below.

Before	After

Were the emotions that you felt before your act of theft rational or irrational? Please explain.

_____
_____
_____
_____
_____
_____
_____
_____
_____
_____
_____
_____
_____
_____
_____
_____
_____
_____
_____
_____
_____
_____
_____
_____
_____
_____
_____
_____

SHOPLIFTING AND THEFT ASSESSMENT

1. Describe your last shoplifting or theft experience.

_____

_____

_____

_____

2. Why did you do it?

_____

_____

_____

_____

3. Did you get caught?   Y or N

_____

_____

_____

_____

4. How did it make you feel afterward? (Circle any that apply)

_____

_____

_____

_____

Guilty	Rush or High	Numb	Neutral Proud	Sly	
Intelligent	Deceptive	Energized	Fearful	Sneaky	Nervous
Thrilled	Happy	Capable	Excited Ashamed	Remorseful	

Other(s): _____

5. How were you feeling prior to the incident?

_____

_____

_____

_____

6. Was this your first time shoplifting or stealing?

    Y or N

7. Was this your first time getting caught? If not, how many times have you been caught?

_____

_____

_____

_____

8. How old were you when you first started shoplifting/stealing?

_____

_____

_____

_____

9. Describe your very first shoplifting/theft experience?

_____

_____

_____

_____

10. Why did you do it?

_____

_____

_____

_____

11. Did you get caught?

    Y or N

12. How did it make you feel?

Guilty	Rush or High	Numb		Neutral	Proud	Sly
Intelligent	Deceptive		Energized	Fearful	Sneaky	Nervous
Thrilled	Happy Capable		Excited Ashamed	Remorseful		

Other(s): _____

13. How does it feel to get caught?

_____

_____

_____

_____

14. How does it feel to get away with it?

_____

_____

_____

_____

15. Are you able to stop shoplifting or stealing if you want?

   Y or N

16. Have you ever tried to stop shoplifting or engaging in other acts of theft? If so, how many times and how long did each period last?

_____

_____

_____

_____

17. Do you steal because you need the item(s) or you want the item(s)?

_____

_____

_____

_____

18. Would you say stealing is a habit or addiction?   Y or N

_____

_____

19. What rewards do you get from shoplifting or stealing?

_____

_____

_____

_____

20. How would you rank your self-esteem?

    1 = Poor

    2 = Fair

    3 = Good

    4 = Very Good

    5 = Excellent

21. Does shoplifting or stealing help relieve any of the following? (Circle any that apply)

    Anxiety   Depression   Frustration

    Feelings of Deprivation   Anger   Boredom

22. Do you sometimes feel like you need or deserve a reward or a gift to lift your spirits?

    Y or N

23. Do you sometimes feel anxiety over your financial situation?

    Y or N

24. Does stealing make you feel in control?

    Y or N

25. Do you feel you give a lot to others but get nothing in return?

    Y or N

26. Do you know anyone else who shoplifts or commits acts of theft?

    Y or N

27. Do you feel like the pull to shoplift or steal is too strong to resist?

    Why or why not?

_____

_____

28. Do you see your shoplifting or stealing as a problem? Why or why not?

_____

_____

_____

_____

29. Are you experiencing any stressful life circumstances?

    Y or N

If yes, pleases explain.

_____

_____

_____

_____

30. Would you describe yourself as any of the following? (Circle all that apply)

Thrill Seeking　　　Depressed　　　　　　　Anxious

Influenced by Peers　　　Frustrated　　　　　　Angry

Poor Coping Skills　　　Impulsive　　　　　　Competitive

31. What are the odds that you will shoplift or steal again?

1 = Will not happen

2 = Might happen

3 = Likely to happen

4 = Very likely to happen

5 = Sure to happen

32. How important is it to you to stop shoplifting or committing acts of theft?

1 = Unimportant

2 = Slightly important

3 = Important

4 = Very important

5 = Critical

WHAT DOES RESEARCH SAY?

According to research, the top two reasons why people steal or shoplift are due to anger and depression. Our objective in group is to learn how to control our emotions.

Many people shoplift or steal for different reasons. Below is a list of why some people choose to commit acts of theft.

- ✓ Anger
- ✓ Depression
- ✓ Anxiety
- ✓ Stress
- ✓ Grief
- ✓ Feeling that life is unfair
- ✓ Competition
- ✓ Low Self-Esteem
- ✓ Wanting to be accepted or fit in
- ✓ To feel power or have control over something
- ✓ Boredom
- ✓ To gain excitement, feel a rush, or feel alive
- ✓ Shame

- ✓ Entitlement (i.e., I deserve a reward or gift because I do so much for others)
- ✓ Rebellion or initiation
- ✓ Greed
- ✓ Lack of patience; looking for a quick fix or solution (does not practice delayed gratification)
- ✓ Societal influences (i.e., keeping up with the Joneses)
- ✓ To pay for drug or gambling habits (addiction issues)
- ✓ Poor financial planning and professional development
- ✓ Desperate (back is against the wall)
- ✓ To make a living (Professional Boosters)

OVERCOMING DEPRESSION

Music – Listen to enjoyable music. Listening to your favorite songs can improve your mood. Music is a powerful tool that has been used in movies to enhance emotions of fear, joy, sadness, excitement, etc. Imagine watching a scary movie without background music or sound effects. It wouldn't be as scary. You can use music to change your mood.

Nostalgia – Reminisce about happy times in your past. Review old pictures, movies, or television series that you used to enjoy. Do things that you used to enjoy, that you don't do now.

Self-Care – Take care of yourself. Get a massage, pedicure, manicure, etc. Go on vacation and eat healthy food. Exercise to increase your production of endorphins. With high endorphin levels, we feel less pain and fewer negative effects of stress. Endorphins have been suggested as modulators of the so-called "runner's high" that athletes achieve with prolonged exercise.

Self-Talk – Monitor or be mindful of what you say to yourself. Try to be positive and say things to yourself that uplift you instead of bring you down. Negative self-talk is not healthy and can destroy your life.

Journaling – Write down what is on your mind. By journaling, you can evaluate your life and express yourself honestly. Act out your emotions on paper. Later, you can review your entries and decide if you were being rational or being irrational. You can review your journal to remind yourself of previous accomplishments, lessons, and how you have overcome obstacles. Journaling is a great tool for personal growth.

Change Environment – Some people live, work, or go to school in negative environments. You would be surprised how exposure to different people, places, or things can improve your life. If you are in a negative environment, consider changing it to a positive one. Your odds of living a happy life increase when you are in a positive environment.

Seek Advice- Receiving guidance from a neutral party who has no emotional attachment to the situation may bring clarity.

Use Stress Prevention Strategies – Do things ahead of time in order to prevent future stressful events from occurring. We want you to anticipate needs. Examples include: budgeting, planning ahead, paying bills on time, leaving early from work to avoid traffic, getting things done before you are asked, telling people "no," etc.

Drawing, Coloring, and Puzzles - Drawing and coloring is extremely relaxing for many. Puzzles can take your focus off of negativity and onto something else. Remember that the things that we used to do as children, we probably still like doing now. We just have forgotten about them.

Sunlight - Taking a walk in nature can improve your mood. Exposure to sunlight has been proven to help people feel better.

Reading - Take your mind off things and read a good book. Many times our mood sucks because we are bored. Magazines, comic books, newspapers are also good options.

Change your medication -Sometimes our medications can have us feeling weird and out of whack. Many medications have side effects that can affect us psychologically.

Change your physiology - Sometimes we just need to get moving. Stand up straight, jump around, smile, make weird faces, stretch, twist etc.

Counseling – Sometimes people become overwhelmed and are unable to cope with life's stressors. If this is the case for you, consider seeing a counselor. A professional counselor can assist you with challenging issues in your life.

Change your focus-stop focusing on your problems and focus on your solutions. Or simply redirect your energy or focus onto something else.

Things that can influence your mood

Caffeine

Food

Pictures

Scents

Hunger

Thirst

Clothes

Heat

Noise

Music

Silence

Looking Good

Looking Bad

Brightness

Dimness

Humor

People

Rest

Events

Colors

Exercise

Finances

(Dis) Satisfaction with life

Grooming

Cleanliness

Body Image

Sex

Health

Love

Stress/Pressure

Animals

Children

Accomplishment

Someone else's vibes

Nostalgia

Massage

Color

Puzzles

Adversity

Opportunity

Injustice

Prejudice

Alcohol

Drugs

Gambling

Shopping/Shoplifting

Winning

Losing

EMOTIONAL INTELLIGENCE

Emotional intelligence (EI) is the ability to perceive, control and evaluate emotions in yourself and others. EI is also ability to understand verbal and nonverbal communication that is presented in any given situation. You can use perception, self-awareness, and mood management strategies to make the right decisions, at the right place, at the right times, to excel in life. The first step is to learn how to manage your mood. Please provide positive solutions to the situations listed below.

When you are annoyed you will do this to improve your mood

_____

_____

When you are angry you will do this to improve your mood

_____

_____

When you are depressed you will do this to improve your mood

_____

_____

When you are disrespected you are going to do this to improve your mood

_____

_____

When you don't feel like exercising you're going to do this to put you in the mood

_____

_____

When you don't feel like taking out the trash you're going to do this to put you in the mood

_____

_____

When you feel like using alcohol or drugs you are going to do this to change your mood

_____

_____

When you don't feel like controlling your mouth you're going to do this to change your mood

_____

_____

When you are bored you are going to do this to keep your mind occupied

_____

_____

When you don't feel like studying you're going to do this to change your mood

_____

_____

When you don't feel like going to work you're going to do this to change your mood

_____

_____

When you are sleepy and you need to wake up, you are going to do this

_____

_____

When you are lonely you are going to make this healthy choice

_____

_____

When you are low on money, you are going to make this positive choice

_____

_____

When your heart is broken you're going to this to feel better

_____

_____

When you're running late you're going to do this to feel better

_____

_____

Add your own personal scenarios below that may occur in your life. After you write them, write down how you are going to deal with them in a healthy manner.

_____

_____

SOCIAL AWARENESS

Write down some things that you notice about society. I call them patterns of life. Knowing certain patterns, tendencies, and behaviors can be advantageous to your personal and professional life, if you pay attention.

For example:

1. The higher the lotto, the more people play.

2. Birds of a feather, flock together.

3. Comfort is addicting.

4. People love instant gratification.

5. Negativity is contagious.

6. Word travels fast.

SELF-AWARENESS

1. What makes you feel happy, relaxed, and fulfilled?

_____

_____

_____

_____

2. What can you do that will instantly change your mood from negative to positive? Really think about it.

_____

_____

_____

_____

3. What are your strengths? Are there other skills that you need to develop? If so, what are they?

_____

_____

_____

_____

4. What are your natural tendencies or habits? What are your behavior patterns? What do you no matter what, every single day?

_____

_____

_____

_____

5. What do you want to be known for? What kind of legacy will you leave behind?

_____

_____

_____

_____

6. Describe the characteristics of your ideal mate. What kind of personality does he/she have? What are his/her physical characteristics? What are deal breakers for you?

Personality	Physical Features	Deal Breakers	Other

7. What was the best birthday you ever had? What did you do and who was there?

_____

_____

_____

_____

8. Who do you admire and respect? What qualities do they have and what do you need to do to get those same qualities?

1. Name: _____ Relationship: _____

Qualities: _____

2. Name: _____ Relationship: _____

Qualities: _____

9. If you could be any fictional character, who would you be and why?

_____

_____

_____

_____

10. If you had a million dollars right now, how would you spend or invest it? Be specific.

_____

_____

_____

_____

SELF-ACTUALIZATION

Create a plan and write down the things that you can do now to become your ideal self.

_____
_____
_____
_____
_____
_____
_____
_____
_____
_____

What would your ideal day consist of?

_____
_____
_____
_____
_____
_____
_____
_____
_____
_____
_____

CRAVINGS

Cravings can start from a bad feeling that you want to escape. Anxiety builds and the desire to steal grows. Urges grow and there is a desire to release the anxiety to feel better. Stealing becomes compulsive because it feels good and can satisfy emotional needs and serve as immediate gratification. Here are the phases that one might go through when being tempted to steal.

Phase 1 – Depression, anxiety, stress, anger, grief, etc.

Phase 2 – Desire to release the bad feeling

Phase 3 – Fantasizing about stealing or the emotional lift it may give

Phase 4 – The urge to steal grows

Phase 5 – Rationalizing theft behavior

Phase 6 – Planning to steal

Phase 7 – Committing an act of theft or shoplifting

We want you to take control of your behavior in the early phases before your urges are too strong.

DEVELOP A PLAN

If you want to be successful in life or recovery, you are going to need to develop a plan. Know what steps you will need to take to get to your goal. Even if you don't write them down, at least know what your plans are. Set deadlines and be actively in pursuit of benchmarks. Check your progress, make adjustments and seek advice to make sure that you are on the right path.

Get organized. Know where everything is. There is nothing worse than scrambling and searching for information when you need it the most. It creates panic and confusion. This can lead to mistakes and wasted time.

One time I had to go dumpster diving because I inadvertently threw away my passport while I was searching for documents in a crisis situation. I ended up frustrated and stressed out. To make things worse, I was anointed with dumpster juice for my lack of organization and preparation. This will never happen again.

I believe that we, as humans, are the most comfortable when we are stable. Most of us find comfort in knowing what is going to happen in the future. Stability gives us a sense of security.

Many children who are moved around from home to home and school to school are known to have behavioral issues. Why is this? They desire stability. Defense mechanisms develop due to fear and emotional instability. Losing friends and leaving a familiar place to move to a strange new environment can be stressful and very scary.

So how do we overcome this sense of instability? We get organized. We bring stability into our lives by developing a schedule and creating a daily regimen. We develop discipline by following our regimen and find comfort in knowing what we are supposed to do and what to expect next. Some of the greatest athletes, military leaders and businessmen of all time were known to follow a regimen. If it helped them, it can help you.

We are groomed to follow a schedule. Most of us have followed a schedule from Kindergarten through the 12th grade. We follow schedules at work, at school and in the military. Prisoners even follow schedules. A schedule gives us structure and stability. We know what to expect and we are mentally prepared for it.

After high school some people begin to experience troubles because they are no longer following a schedule. Some would say that they have lost their structure and discipline. Maybe this is why some people go into the military. They may want to improve their personal development by entering a structured program that provides discipline while they are proudly serving their country.

Throughout life, you have to realize that you are going to have to jump through some hoops to get where you want to be. This journey will not be easy. People and situations are going to try to stop you from reaching your goal. This is where wisdom and preparation come into play. Always have a backup plan for every scenario. We call this a Relapse Prevention Plan.

Create a desired response or action for every challenging scenario that you may face. The goal is to prevent yourself from going back to your previous undesired behaviors. The prevention plan keeps you on track.

For example, let's say you are trying to sell someone some cookies and they tell you, "I am not interested in buying cookies." Your prevention plan for this response could be to keep a smile on your face and say, "Not a problem, here are some free samples and some coupons just in case you decide to change your mind. Have a good day." And move on to the next person. Having planned responses or actions for different scenarios puts you at an advantage mentally. Rejection becomes more tolerable the more you practice dealing with it. In addition it makes you look powerful when you approach a person without fear and handle rejection well. It gives off the impression that you are confident and have a million options.

Don't go back to your old behaviors or lose your vision or confidence because you get rejected. It happens, and it's a part of life. Remember, rejection can sometimes be a test. People will test you to see how you react to certain situations.

Customer service is a dying art. I appreciate excellent customer service and so do other people. If they see you get an attitude after they turn you down, they will never buy from you in the future. Money is precious these days and no one will want to give their hard-earned money to someone with an attitude problem. This means that you were being phony in the first place.

Rejection can turn into an opportunity. Let's play through this scenario again. The customer tells you, "I am not interested in buying cookies." You then ask the customer, "Well, what are you interested in buying?" Whoa! The door of opportunity just opened. Do you see the difference? You might have some almonds that the customer is interested in buying. Who knows?

Small accomplishments build confidence. The more you accomplish, the more confident you become. The more experience you have, the more confident you become. Experience combined with accomplishments builds confidence.

RELAPSE PREVENTION PLAN

Relapse Prevention Plans are created to assist in monitoring behavior patterns and gives you the ability to make adjustments. This tool will assist you in examining your behavior and creating positive alternative choices when you are triggered to shoplift or commit acts of theft. Please write down your triggers and your usual response to them. After that is complete, write down the same triggers and a positive alternative response for each trigger.

Trigger	Negative Response
Example: Failure	Response: Go to the store and steal something

Trigger	Negative Response
Example: Failure	Response: I'm going to view this as a learning process and I understand that many people fail. Now is not the time to be irrational and steal something. I will take a break and do something that improves my mood. When I am ready, I will try again.

AVOIDING TRIGGERS

You may have heard some people that are in recovery say "be smart, not strong." This implies that we can avoid returning to negative behavior patterns by using better judgment. If we are smart, we do not have to be strong. Certain people, places, or things can trigger negative behavior patterns or relapse. By placing yourself in these situations, it will require you to be strong. Many of us think we are strong, but we are really not. Choose to be smart and avoid your triggers.

In the boxes below, please list the people, places, and things that you need to avoid.

People	Places	Things

PERCEPTION

How we view or see things can influence our thought process and behavior. Inaccurate perceptions of situations can lead to negative thinking, negative behavior, and negative consequences. There is power in perception. Have you ever viewed something as hard to achieve and then when you tried it, it was easy? Or have you ever viewed something as easy and it was actually hard? Or have you ever had the wrong perception of someone or something? We have to be mindful of our perceptions. Everything is not always what it seems to be and we need to make sure that we are looking through the right lens.

1. What is your perception of being in this group? Please be honest.

_____
_____
_____
_____

2. How did you come to this conclusion? Is it based on your personal experience or what others have told you?

_____
_____
_____
_____

3. Do you have the right perception? Are you looking through the right lens?

_____
_____
_____
_____

4. Many people say that "seeing is believing." Is this true or false? Please explain.

_____
_____
_____
_____

The statement "seeing is believing" is based on perception. There are those that will never manage their anger because they don't see themselves having a problem. They will rationalize or defend their behavior because they perceive it as acceptable. They may even believe or perceive that others are the ones with the real problem.

5. What perception do you have of yourself? What do you believe about yourself? Please be honest.

_____

_____

_____

_____

6. Sometimes having the wrong perception can trigger people lose control of their emotions. Has this ever happened to you? If so, what can you do to reduce wrong perceptions?

_____

_____

_____

_____

7. Have you ever perceived something as a crisis and it really wasn't? Describe what happened.

_____

_____

_____

_____

8. What can you do to make sure you make rational choices?

_____

_____

_____

_____

9. Many say, "I don't care what other people think." But many are lying to themselves. What strategies can you use to keep a positive mindset if someone perceives you the wrong way?

_____

_____

_____

_____

_____

_____

_____

_____

10. If you failed to manage your anger on a regular basis what would be the possible consequences?

_____

_____

_____

_____

What did you learn from this situation?

_____

_____

_____

_____

Denial is something that we must discuss in this group. There are those in group that will not admit that they committed an act of theft or shoplifting, when they know they did. Others will rationalize their behavior and defend their choices. Most of them know what they are saying is full of you-know-what. They are not fooling the counselor or the people around them.

With this being said...What are you in denial about? Denial can lead to negative consequences. Here are a list of things that some people are in denial about:

Addiction   Finances

Relationships   Career Choice

Eating Habits   Fame

Getting Older   Spending Habits

Exercising   Illness

Family History   Work Ethic

School Work   Children

Personality   Appearance

1. Can you add to this list? What are people in denial about?

_____

_____

_____

_____

2. Why do you think some people live in denial?

_____

_____

_____

_____

3. Is this healthy?

Yes or No

4. What are you in denial about? Are you going to stay in denial or change?

_____

_____

_____

_____

5. Does denial truly help you? Please explain

_____

_____

_____

_____

6. What would you like to change? Put a check next to all that apply to you.

___ Substance Use	___ Excessive Spending
___ Financial Management	___ Spouse
___ Peer Group	___ Physical Health
___ Abusive Behavior	___ Career
___ Jealousy and Envy	___ Work Environment
___ Resentment	___ Self-Talk
___ Commitment	___ Values
___ Decision Making	___ Education Level
___ Temperament	___ Thought Process
___ Discipline	___ Criminal Behavior
___ Mental Health	___ Theft
___ Shoplifting	___ Check Fraud
___ Negative Thinking	___ Embezzlement

STAGES OF CHANGE

Stage 1: Pre-contemplation (Not Ready)

Individuals do not see their behavior as a problem in this stage. Those in the Pre-contemplation stage do not intend to take action in the foreseeable future, even if they have experienced negative consequences for their actions.

Stage 2: Contemplation (Getting Ready)

Contemplation is the stage in which people are aware of the pros and cons of changing their behavior. Instead of defending their behavior, they evaluate, and consider the idea of changing. Continuously weighing the costs and benefits of changing can produce chronic contemplation or procrastination.

Stage 3: Preparation

Preparation is the stage to take action and do specific things that promote change. These individuals have a plan of action, such as going to therapy, talking to their physician, buying a self-help book, scheduling, creating a budget, etc.

Stage 4: Action

Action is the stage in which people have made specific, overt modifications in their lifestyles. Observers from the outside, like friends, relatives, and co-workers will notice that change is occurring. Specific actions are taken to promote lifestyle changes.

Stage 5: Maintenance

Maintenance is the stage in which people have made positive lifestyle choices and have been successful at avoiding relapse. While in the Maintenance stage, people are less tempted to relapse and grow increasingly more confident that they can continue their changes.

What stage of change are you in for the selection that applied to you?

___ Substance Use	___ Discipline
___ Financial Management	___Mental Health
___ Peer Group	___Shoplifting
___ Abusive Behavior	___Check Fraud
___ Jealousy and Envy	___Negative Thinking
___ Resentment	___ Excessive Spending
___ Commitment	___ Spouse
___ Decision Making	___ Physical Health
___ Temperament	___ Career

___ Work Environment   ___ Thought Process

___ Self-Talk   ___ Criminal Behavior

___ Values   ___ Theft

___ Education Level   ___ Embezzlement

How can you improve your weak areas?

_____

_____

_____

_____

MOTIVATION TO CHANGE

Many people minimize their behavior, make multiple excuses, or say "Why should I change?" Motivation to change usually occurs when there is a perceived purpose or benefit to change.

For example:

- Quitting your current job, for a new job, that pays more money and offers more benefits.
- Breaking up with your spouse because your future will be better without them.
- Buying a new car, because the one you have keeps breaking down.

In this section, we want you to weigh the long-term pros and cons of changing your behavior.

Pros	Cons

Pros	Cons

SELF-ESTEEM

Self-esteem is a term in psychology to reflect a person's overall evaluation or appraisal of his or her own worth. Low self-esteem affects both males and females.

1. How does someone with low self-esteem act?

_____

_____

_____

_____

2. How does someone with healthy self-esteem act?

_____

_____

_____

_____

3. What is the difference between healthy self-esteem and arrogance?

_____

_____

_____

_____

4. Sometimes those with low self-esteem try to bully, abuse, or talk down to others. Why do you think they do this? Have you ever experienced this? If so, how did this affect you or others?

_____

_____

_____

5. How do you deal with bullies at the workplace?

_____

_____

_____

_____

Strategies to Improve Self-Esteem

✓ Pursue easy goals

Start with something you can accomplish easily. When we achieve small successes, it builds our confidence and momentum to go after bigger goals.

✓ Socialize

Get out of the house and practice your communication and interpersonal skills. Don't be afraid to engage in conversations. Others may be just as nervous as we are and do not express it. We are not alone. Some people are magicians and we only see what they allow us to see.

✓ Face your fears

It is important for us to face our fears so we can grow. By repeatedly facing our fears our irrational beliefs diminish and we gain confidence and courage.

✓ Build on your strengths

Do things on a regular basis that comes natural for you. Doing things that you are good at reinforces belief in your abilities and strengths. You can also add to your skills by taking advanced coursework or certification training in your field of study.

✓ Stop comparing yourself to others

Stop comparing yourself to other people. Low self-esteem stems from the feeling of being inferior. For example, if you were the only person in the world, do you think you could have low self-esteem? Self-esteem only comes into the picture when there are other people around us and we perceive that we are inferior. Don't worry about what your neighbor is doing. Accept that it'll serve you more to just go down your own path at your own pace rather than to compare yourself.

✓ Know thyself

Know who you are and what you need to improve on. Your self-esteem is based on the major categories of your life. Write down all the major categories of your life (e.g., health, finance, relationships, etc.). Then rate yourself on a scale of 1-10 in each area. Work on the lowest numbered category first. Each area affects the other areas. The more you build up each area of your life, the higher your overall self-esteem.

✓ Create a vision of yourself

Use your imagination and create an image of yourself as the confident and self-assured person you aspire to become. When you are this person, how will you feel? How will others perceive you? What does your body language look like? How will you talk? Feel the emotions, experiences, and daydream about your ideal life.

✓ Help others achieve their goals

Helping others achieve their goals can be fulfilling. It puts a smile on their face and can make you feel good as well. Plus if you help them with their goals, maybe they will help you with your goals.

✓ Create a plan

Having a goal is not enough. You need to have an action plan. Get moving and follow the steps that you need to take to achieve your goals.

✓ Get motivated

Be purpose driven. Have a reason why you are doing something. Associate yourself with people or things that inspire you. If you desire to be motivated, use this formula: High Emotion + Strong Purpose = Motivation

✓ Improve self-talk

Sometimes we have internal thoughts that are negative and irrational. We have to manage our self-talk and reinforce positive thoughts that improve our perspective. Internally, we can say good things about ourselves and build a positive image.

✓ Be positive

There are many people that allow negative energy to transfer into their lives. Know that it is okay to smile and people are attracted to happy people. Do not allow negative people to transfer their energy into you. Just because they are mad does not mean that you have to be. You are in control of your perceptions. There are no benefits to being negative.

PERSONAL ADVICE

Imagine that you are five years in the future and you have to write a letter to your present self. What advice would you give?

_____

_____

_____

_____

_____

_____

_____

_____

_____

_____

_____

_____

_____

_____

_____

_____

_____

_____

_____

_____

_____

_____

_____

_____

FORGIVENESS

Forgiveness is one of the hardest things to do. Letting go of the past and removing resentment is healthy. There are no benefits to holding on to grudges and past drama. It's like driving a car while looking through the rearview mirror the entire time. Eventually, you will crash.

1. Who do you need to forgive and why?

Family   Friends Co-workers   Spouse   Children   Yourself

_____

_____

_____

_____

2. Do you forgive and forget? Or do you forgive and not forget?

_____

_____

_____

_____

3. Is making amends important to you? If so, who do you need to say sorry to, and why?

_____

_____

_____

_____

4. What does true forgiveness look, act, and sound like?

_____

_____

_____

5. After you forgive someone, does that mean you should still associate yourself with them?

_____

_____

_____

_____

APOLOGY LETTER

Write a letter to the person that you want forgiveness from.

_____
_____
_____
_____
_____
_____
_____
_____
_____
_____
_____
_____
_____
_____
_____
_____
_____
_____
_____
_____
_____
_____
_____
_____
_____

LIVING BY PRINCIPLES

It is important to have principles. Principles are the governors of your values and protect the things that you care about the most. The principles that you create will help you when you need to make tough decisions.

Values

Freedom

Principle: I do not commit acts of theft or shoplifting.

This protects my freedom and keeps me out of jail.

Career

Principle: I attend trainings quarterly to improve my skill level.

This helps my career and shows that I am committed.

Reputation

Principle: I have a strong work ethic and provide quality service.

This protects my reputation and increases my earning potential.

List the things that you value.

1._____

2._____

3._____

4._____

Now write down principles that protect those values.

1._____

_____

_____

2._____

_____

_____

3._____

_____

4.

BELIEF AND SELF-IMAGE

You have to believe that you can accomplish anything that you are trying to achieve. This is the link in the chain that many people miss. They go after their goals, but secretly believe that they will not achieve them. They are lukewarm and passive instead of being on fire and pro-active. They lack confidence and continue to second guess themselves due to fear and a damaged self-image.

Self-image is extremely important. If a man sees a woman that he is interested in dating and physically she is rated a ten and he is a five, the likelihood of him approaching her is slim to none. His tendency will be to approach women that are closer to his physical rating of five. But if he feels like a ten internally and has great self-esteem, he will not have a problem approaching the woman.

I have talked to many women who people would consider tens physically and noticed that their self-image was low. Because of their education level, family and abuse history they ranked themselves as a four or below. They limited their options based on their skewed self-image and involved themselves in relationships with people who were fours and below ethically, morally, physically, and spiritually. From the outside looking in, I used to ask myself "What do they see in those guys? They could do way better." But they never will, until their self-image improves.

Have you ever worked with an over-worked, under-paid, and under-appreciated co-worker who was reliable, talented and possessed a strong work ethic? Did you ever wonder why they accepted poor treatment from their employer? In many instances, people accept this treatment as a result of their poor self-image. They do not feel that they truly deserve better and do not know their worth or true value. This applies to personal and professional relationships as well.

The majority of people do not have the faith to apply for a job that is paying $100,000 a year if they are currently making $30,000 a year. Being hired for a job that pays $100,000 a year is not believable for them. Why? Because they don't believe that they are qualified or worth $100,000 per year; therefore, they will not apply for $100,000 a year job even though there are thousands of these positions available. They will question themselves and allow doubt to fill their awareness. Their self-image or programming cannot accept a $100,000 a year salary thus they will apply for a job that pays $35,000 a year because that is what they are comfortable with. It does not take a lot of faith to apply for a job that pays $5,000 more than what they are currently earning. The ability to earn $100,000 per year is out of the question in their minds. Why do they think this way? It is because of their self-image and belief system. They are allowing the programming of their past or current situation to affect their future. In essence, they are influenced by the dominating beliefs of their family, friends, teachers, co-workers, and employers to infiltrate their psyche and influence their self-image or self-worth.

You would be surprised by the number of people that do not achieve happiness because they fail to change their self-image. Some people say they want a new car but they are too scared to visit the car lot and check the price. The sad reality is, some of them can afford it! They ASSUME their way out of their dream with negativity and fear. Don't let this happen to you. I want you to know that you are valuable and worthy. You have to believe in yourself and believe that you can achieve your dreams.

So how do you improve your self-image? You start by believing in yourself and start thinking about what you truly want. Write down what you really want to experience in your life with no limitations. Then you work on improving your value through education, working out, changing environments, and associating yourself with people of higher value. You change your self-talk and think positively instead of negatively and appreciate what you do have. Be thankful and repetitively tell yourself that your dreams are possible and start looking for opportunities. Do positive things that you enjoy and stimulate your mind. Your daily goal is to feel good, be happy and always put yourself in a position to where you perform masterfully.

On a daily basis I want you to visualize yourself achieving your dream on a huge movie theatre screen. Make this experience as vivid and emotionally compelling as possible. You should be able to describe what everything smells like, looks like, and feels like. You need to be emotionally involved during this visualization process. I highly recommend that you have a graphic designer make a customized vision board for you. The vision board will include your picture and life-like Photo-shopped images that create a scene of you accomplishing your dream. Put this on your wall and look at it every day. Or have it saved as a screensaver on your cell phone.

Write down good things about yourself and read them daily. Avoid watching negative programing that makes you upset, nervous, or fearful. I believe in being informed, but I try to avoid watching the news as much as possible. Watch and listen to things that make you feel good, happy and optimistic.

I cannot sugarcoat this process. This is going to take work because you are competing with years of negative programing. Many people know this stuff but few choose to practice it because it requires work, discipline, time, and belief. This is a daily repetitive process that is designed to reprogram you to be optimistic, secure, and confident.

What is your overall view of yourself physically, emotionally, and intellectually?

Physically I am:

_____   _____

_____   _____

_____   _____

_____   _____

Emotionally I am:

_____   _____

_____   _____

_____   _____

_____   _____

Intellectually I am:

_____   _____

_____   _____

_____   _____

_____   _____

Spiritually I am:

_____   _____

_____   _____

_____   _____

Write down a list of "shoulds" that you have based on your family, friends, culture, spirituality, media, music, school system, and any other areas. Which of these beliefs are rational and which are irrational? Place an "R" next the beliefs that you think are rational and an "I" next to the beliefs that you deem irrational. Place an "X" next to the statements that describe who you are currently.

		R or I	I am
Example:	I should be skinny	__R__	__X__
	I should be perfect	__I__	_____
	I should be married by now	__I__	_____
I should get all A's		__R__	_____
I should _____		_____	_____
I should _____		_____	_____
I should _____		_____	_____
I should _____		_____	_____
I should _____		_____	_____
I should _____		_____	_____
I should _____		_____	_____
I should _____		_____	_____
I should _____		_____	_____
I should _____		_____	_____
I should _____		_____	_____

Write down as many great things about yourself that you can think of in the next 2 minutes.

_____

_____

_____

_____

_____

_____

_____

_____

_____

_____

_____

_____

_____

Write down as many not-so-great things about yourself that you can think of in the next 2 minutes.

_____

_____

_____

_____

_____

_____

_____

_____

_____

_____

_____

_____

Now analyze your two lists. Was it more difficult to write one list than the other? Which list is longer? Why do you think that is?

_____

_____

_____

_____

_____

Write a list of things that people have told you about yourself. Place an "X" next to the statements that you either agree or disagree with.

Example: Agree   Disagree

I am an excellent writer.   __X__   _____

I am lazy.   __X__   _____

_____   _____   _____

_____   _____   _____

_____   _____   _____

_____   _____   _____

_____   _____   _____

_____   _____   _____

Write a list of things that you believe people think about you. Place an "X" next to the statements that you either agree or disagree with.

Finish the following statement:

People believe that I am: Agree   Disagree

_____   _____   _____

_____   _____   _____

_____   _____   _____

_____   _____   _____

_____   _____   _____

_____   _____   _____

Do other's thoughts about you determine your future? Or do your thoughts about yourself determine your future? _____

LET IT GO

No matter how old you are or how many times you have failed, I want you to understand that the show isn't over. One of my clients told me that he was 46 and he was too old to go back to school and try new things. I replied to him, "The average male lives to the age of 76 in the United States so you have 30 more years to make something happen." If you don't do it for yourself, do it for your family.

Playtime is over and you have adult bills and adult responsibilities. There has to be a sense of urgency because time is flying by. We can make up for our mistakes in the past by working on our future. I used to tell everyone when I was 34 that I was making up for all of the mistakes that I made when I was 17. I was living my second 17 and I had the opportunity to learn from my mistakes and make the right choices.

Some of us are still living in the past and need to let it go. If you cannot let it go, at least make up for it with your actions today. Do not fail the same tests over and over again. Some would describe that as insanity. We have the ability to move forward and start a new career, develop new goals and pursue what we want in life. Age should never limit us.

If you are seasoned in age, I would say that you are ahead of the game because you have a lifetime of experiences to pull from. You already know what doesn't work. So it is your job not to do those things and try something different. In addition, you probably know what you want out of life and what you will accept. You have a better sense of direction than a younger person. Chances are that you have serious responsibilities that cannot be taken lightly. Your sense of urgency is more intense and you are less likely to procrastinate. Time is of importance and you don't have the patience to tolerate foolishness.

You are an asset to the community because you have a deeper understanding of issues and a memory bank that is loaded with information. All you have to do is tap into your mental vault and make withdrawals of experience before you make decisions. Many times you have the ability to predict behavior and foresee the outcomes of future events because of your age. This is what makes you great.

1. What is the purpose of holding on to the past?

_____

_____

_____

_____

2. Where does "holding on to the past" get you?

_____

_____

_____

_____

3. Is your past affecting you presently? If so, how?

_____

_____

_____

_____

4. Does holding on to negative things in your past benefit you in any way?

_____

_____

_____

_____

5. Seriously, does being negative or pessimistic lead to positive results?

_____

_____

_____

_____

6. If no, why do people continue to do it?

_____

_____

_____

_____

7. What are the characteristics of victims?

_____

_____

_____

_____

8. Do those characteristics describe you? Would you like to be held in eternal bondage by your past?

_____

_____

_____

_____

DELAYED GRATIFICATION

1. How has instant gratification affected your life?

_____

_____

_____

2. What are the benefits of delayed gratification?

_____

_____

_____

_____

3. What are the cons of instant gratification?

_____

_____

_____

_____

4. Are fast things good for you? Please explain.

_____

_____

_____

_____

_____

5. Do good things come to those who wait? Please explain.

_____

_____

_____

_____

_____

FEAR

Many are controlled by fear. These fears can manifest into anger, depression, and impulse-control problems. FEAR stands for: false existence appearing real.

Fear is a dream killer. It is also an emotion that protects us from physical and mental harm. Most people do not go after their dreams and goals because they are trying to protect themselves from mental harm. But are their fears really harmful?

You can desensitize yourself from fear if you choose to. We can rise above fear by facing it on a regular basis so it becomes less threatening. Sometimes we fear what we do not understand and become intimidated. This does not have to be the case. We can train our minds to think rationally and our bodies to be calm when faced with fearful situations. Continuous, controlled, safe exposure to fearful situations can desensitize us. Some call this Exposure Therapy.

It is important to find your purpose. But many are scared to find their purpose because they will have the responsibility to live up to it. Others are simply scared of achieving goals because mediocracy has become normalized.

There are instances where students will dumb themselves down in school so that their peers will feel comfortable around them. Is this what we really want? Living in fear is a mental prison that is extremely destructive to our progress as human beings.

You do not have to be controlled by fear. If you are, others will use it against you. Sometimes I embarrass myself on purpose to practice facing my fear. Some may think it is silly, but I don't care. I put myself in situations that can potentially lead to my embarrassment. I am willing to look like a fool in front of others. This creates a shift in my perception. The feeling of embarrassment evaporates because I am continuously facing my fears. I am doing this for my development and conducting social experiments to improve my life. The long-term benefit outweighs the short-term potential laughter.

Sometimes we let opportunities pass us by because we are scared of embarrassment or rejection. If I am faced with an opportunity that requires courage and can positively change my life, I will act on it. Sometimes one has to risk looking like a fool to get ahead in life.

You have to be willing to face rejection. But looking stupid and facing rejection won't matter if you have mastered your mind. Practice facing your fears.

1. What are you really afraid of?

_____

_____

_____

_____

_____

_____

_____

2. What has fear stopped you from doing?

_____

_____

_____

_____

_____

_____

_____

3. How has fear impacted your life?

_____

_____

_____

_____

_____

_____

_____

HOPE

Working to survive and get by is not good enough. You have to fight for your dream and be pro-active. All of this is initiated by hope. If you strip a person of their hope, they have nothing to live for.

Hope is stronger than fear. If you have hope, you will fight for what you believe in. Imagine how this world would be if you stripped it of hope. It would be an extremely miserable place. Now imagine this world without fear. People would be running wild in the streets and there would be mayhem. Fear protects us from unnecessary harm but, it should not consume us. Our hope should outweigh our fear.

Imagine that you are taking a test that you know all of the answers to and a huge, hungry lion is in front of you, chained to a pole, growling at you and licking its chops. How will you do on this test? Will you be able to focus and get all of your answers right? Probably not. This is how fear can stop you from accomplishing your goals. You know all of the answers on the test, but fear can get in the way of your success. This happens every day; the only difference is that there is no lion. The lion is replaced with something else. Get over your fear so that you can pass your test and move to the next level.

You have to hope for more and not settle for anything less than what you are capable of doing. Work toward achieving your potential and fight for what you believe in. You have the ability to achieve as long as you continue dreaming.

There are dream killers out there, and you have to attack them with your confidence. Break their spirit with your passion and enthusiasm. Tell them to go mess with somebody else because they are dealing with someone who is more than a survivor. You are a conqueror and do not tolerate pessimism or negativity in your presence.

Fight for what you believe in and don't be afraid. What would it feel like to leave this life satisfied? Close your eyes and imagine how that would feel right now. I guarantee if you leave this life satisfied, you will be thankful that you chose to be brave.

Satisfaction comes to those who go out and get it. No one is going to give you anything unless you put yourself in the position to get it. Having hope is great, but you have to have actions behind it to achieve want you want. Put yourself in a confident and productive state of mind and achieve your breakthrough.

Nothing can stop you because you have the will and power to move forward and fight, dream, hope and work for your success. Happiness is around the corner and waiting for you to come and get it. All you have to do is attach hope with positive, consistent action and you will find what you are looking for.

You will live what other people dream about. But make sure that after you achieve success, you put your hand back and lift someone else up. Be a guide, a mentor and a help to someone else. We do not achieve success without help from others. Always remember that. Remember who you are and where you came from. Encourage others to chase their happiness, because once they do that, everything else will come.

Chase your happiness until you are out of breath. And if you cannot breathe anymore, find someone else to do the breathing for you. If you cannot find a way, make a way. Do not leave this life saying, "Would have, could have, should have."

CRIMINAL THINKING

There are those in recovery that attempt to "get over" or hustle the system due to criminal thinking. These thinking patterns have been developed over time and may have been introduced by friend, associate, co-worker, or family member. This type of thinking can be considered manipulative, sneaky, hostile, irrational, morally or ethically wrong.

1. Do you have a criminal mind?

Yes or No

2. How does having a criminal mind add or decrease value to one's life?

_____

_____

_____

_____

3. Do you associate yourself with criminals? If so, why?

_____

_____

_____

_____

4. Are you willing to do time for something that someone else did?

_____

_____

_____

_____

_____

_____

_____

_____

5. Do you believe in snitching?

Yes or No

6. Is having a criminal reputation negative or positive?

_____

_____

_____

_____

7. Why is snitching considered to be negative amongst criminals? I thought having a "rap sheet" improves criminal reputation?

_____

_____

_____

_____

8. Is living a criminal lifestyle stress free? What are the potential consequences of living this way?

_____

_____

_____

_____

9. What are the principles that criminals live by? Do these principles protect your values?

_____

_____

_____

_____

_____

10. Many criminals say they don't have any other options and that is why they commit crimes. How is this true when there are examples of people who come from the same circumstances overcoming the same obstacles? Do criminals choose to be victims and make excuses? Or are they as strong as they claim to be?

_____

_____

_____

_____

_____

PENALTIES OF SHOPLIFTING AND THEFT

- ✓ Public humiliation
- ✓ Loss of time
- ✓ Loss of respect
- ✓ Loss of relationships
- ✓ Added stress
- ✓ Probation
- ✓ Community Service
- ✓ Loss of freedom
- ✓ Loss of money
- ✓ Lost opportunities
- ✓ Loss of professional licenses
- ✓ Expulsion from school
- ✓ Diminished reputation
- ✓ Loss of property
- ✓ Criminal record
- ✓ Court fees, fines, etc.
- ✓ Employment loss
- ✓ Loss of citizenship/residency
- ✓ Embarrassment
- ✓ Guilt
- ✓ Trauma
- ✓ Mugshots posted online
- ✓ Arrest

FINANCIAL CONSEQUENCES

Fines $_____

Income lost from not working $_____

Legal Fees (Probation/Court/Lawyer) $_____

Evaluation $_____

Shoplifting/Theft Classes $_____

Childcare $_____

Gas $_____

Food bought while taking classes $_____

Loss of wages $_____

Repair bills or restitution $_____

TOTAL MONEY LOST $_____

Hours in court   _____

Hours in probation   _____

Hours doing community service   _____

Hours in jail   _____

Hours in class   _____

Other hours lost   _____

TOTAL TIME LOST   _____

TIME x HOURLY WAGE = VALUE OF TIME LOST

_____ X $_____ = $_____

VALUE OF TIME LOST $_____

VALUE OF TIME LOST + TOTAL MONEY LOSS= $_____

IS IT WORTH IT? _____

KEEPING UP WITH THE JONESES

Many commit check fraud, embezzlement and other acts of theft to keep up or live a certain lifestyle. These criminal acts have short-term benefits with long-term consequences. There are many who steal to impress others or even pretend to have a lifestyle that they really do not have. Gaining acceptance and approval from others can be intoxicating. We see examples of this behavior played out through social media sites, school yards, clubs, and even the workplace.

This behavior can become burdensome and lead to increased pressure to keep up the lie. This is an unfortunate position to be in for many. This can lead to embarrassment, criminal charges, and addiction. But is it worth it? Do we want people to love us or our lifestyle?

Does our lifestyle define us as a person? Are the clothes, shoes, cars, designer bags, and electronics really important? Are we chasing the lifestyle, or are we really chasing the feeling that the lifestyle gives us? Ask yourself, does another person has less value than another because of the car they drive or the clothes they have? For those that have so-called "nice things," are they really happy or are they wearing a mask?

There are those in those in this world that I call magicians. You see what they want you to see. They don't want you to know who they really are. It's all an illusion and at the end of the magic show nothing changes. Their problems, insecurities, and issues are still there. The clothes, electronics, purses, shoes can temporarily mask the depression, guilt, shame, and anger for a while. But the truth always catches up with them, and it can be revealing.

We are more valuable that clothes, cars, shoes and fancy gadgets. We can replace these things. But no one can replace us. We should not compare ourselves to others because it causes insecurity and you never know what that person is really going through emotionally, physically, or spiritually. They may be paying a price that we are not willing to pay.

I knew a woman who was worth millions at the time I met her, but she was severely unhappy. Her husband was struggling with a methamphetamine addiction and he was having sex with many of her female clients. There was high turnover rate within her organization and her mood and behavior was erratic. This drove her employees crazy and many of them talked negatively behind her back.

Let this be a lesson to all that read this. Happiness is not defined by what we have, it's defined by how we feel. The woman I mentioned above had millions of dollars, respect in the community, and a wonderful lifestyle. But at the end of the day, she was empty inside searching for love, happiness and respect.

We must confront our core issues and not be bullied by our past, false perceptions, and things that don't really matter. It is ok to be vulnerable or exposed. Our lives cannot be based on lies or illusions. Telling the truth has to be more comfortable than telling a lie.

1. Who are better liars? Women or men?

_____

_____

_____

_____

2. How do women lie differently than men? How do they cover it up? What tactics do they use?

_____

_____

_____

3. Do you respect liars? Why or why not?

_____

_____

_____

_____

4. Do you lie to yourself? If so, why?

_____

_____

_____

_____

5. What is a purpose of a lie?

_____

_____

_____

6. How have lies hurt you in the past?

_____

_____

_____

_____

7. Strip away your ego, defenses, and lies you tell yourself. Truly, who are you?

_____

_____

_____

_____

DECISION TREE

In life, we are required to make a lot of decisions, both big and small. Each choice we make will have a ripple effect on many different aspects of our life that we may have failed to consider. This is why it is very important to evaluate our choices in order to create the best possible outcomes.

Creating a decision tree helps you see the possible ripple effects of your choices.

Sample Decision Tree

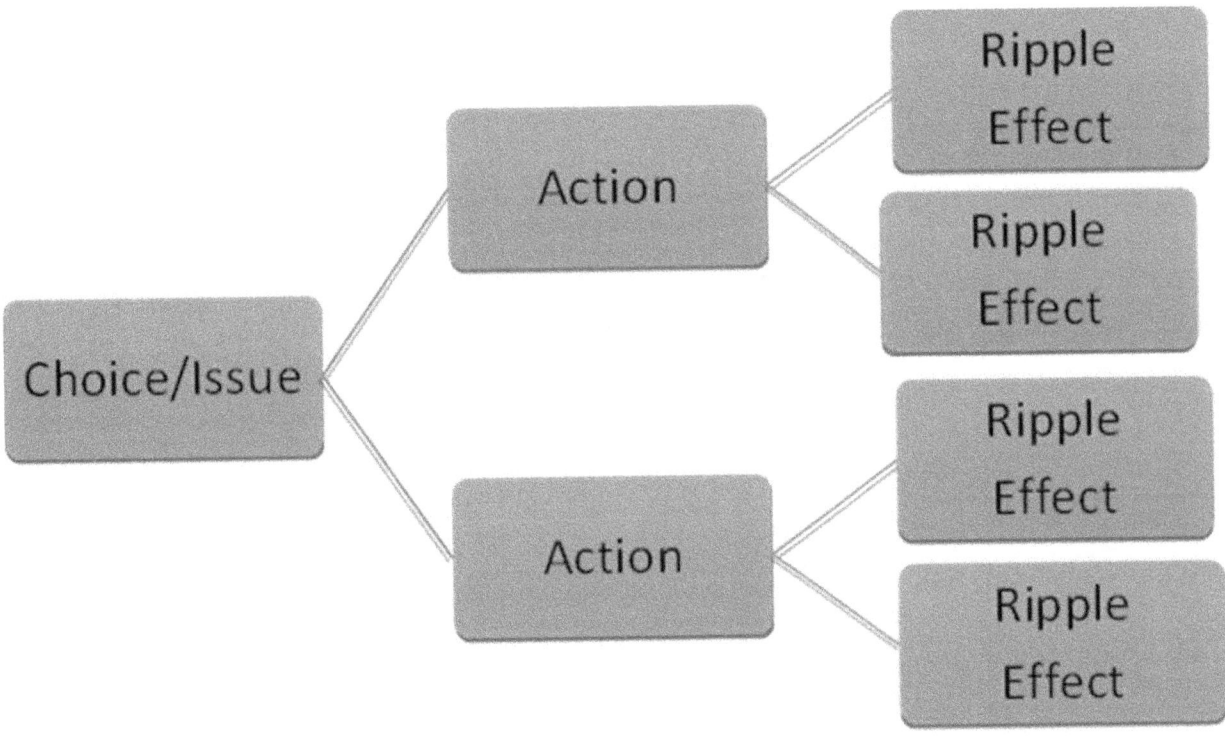

Please create your own decision tree and write down the ripple effects of committing acts of theft.

CREDIT

So what is credit anyway? In essence, credit is any form of delayed payment. It allows one party (the debtor or borrower) to receive money, goods, or services from another party (the creditor or lender) without having to pay up front.

Instead there is an agreement based on trust that the borrower will either pay or return the materials (or other materials of equal value) at a later date. The cost of credit comes in the form of a predetermined rate of interest that is applied to the amount borrowed and will accrue until the debt has been paid.

Credit bureaus collect information from various sources regarding your borrowing and bill-paying habits and create a report based on these findings. A credit score is a number that represents your credit worthiness. It is formulated based on your credit report. The most common credit scores are FICO scores. FICO scores range from 300 – 850. The higher the score, the better your credit. Your credit score is used to determine whether you are worthy of credit, to determine interest rates, and assess your ability to pay back loans. In essence, your past behavior is used to predict your future behavior. Because credit is based on trust and your previous financial behavior, it is very important to create a flawless track record of bill paying activity.

1. Do you know your credit score? If so, what is it?

_____

_____

_____

_____

2. When was the last time you checked your credit score and credit report?

_____

_____

_____

_____

3. Do you typically pay your bills on time? Why or why not?

_____

_____

_____

_____

4. How many lines of credit do you have open (credit cards, loans, etc.)?

_____

_____

_____

_____

5. Are your credit cards maxed out? If so, why?

_____

_____

_____

_____

6. Do you pay the minimum amount allowed? If so, why?

_____

_____

_____

_____

7.How soon do you think you will be able to pay off your credit cards?

_____

_____

_____

_____

8. Do you have a plan in place to pay off your debts? If so, what is it?

_____

_____

_____

_____

9. How can you improve your credit? (FYI, having no credit is bad credit)

_____

_____

_____

_____

SAVE MONEY

It is extremely important to save your money. So many people blow their cash during seasons of overflow. When seasons of famine hit, they regret their previous spending habits.

If you are in the military make sure that you save your money. Don't get caught up going on spending sprees and blowing money in the clubs. I have friends and family that were in the military. Now that they are out, they feel remorse for their actions.

If you are in college, do not go on shopping sprees after you get your refund check. Use that money for rent and school supplies. Likewise, don't go crazy in the mall after you get your paycheck. Remember that you are a student and you should live modestly. This is especially true if the refund check results from a student loan. Remember that you will have to pay that money back with interest. Time flies and soon you will have to pay back those loans.

Try to save at least ten percent of your gross earnings. Create savings goals for yourself and buy books on financial planning and investing. Do things that will allow your money to work for you. List your daily expenses, find out where your money goes and then make the necessary adjustments. Remember that purchases that depreciate in value are not good investments.

Pay yourself before you pay your bills. Get in the habit of saving. Don't lend money that you cannot afford to lose. You do not want it to be a big deal, if you do not receive your money back. This will help to prevent any misunderstandings and ruined relationships over money.

Know the difference between a want and a need. A want is something that you want to have. It may be something frivolous or superficial. A need is something that you absolutely must have to survive. Be sure to take care of the needs first. The wants can wait. Plenty of money is wasted on wants. Remember that you need to invest in your future. Your actions today will determine whether you will have to work well into your seventies, which I'm sure no one wants to do. If saving is hard for you, have a portion of your money automatically drafted into a savings account on a bi-weekly or monthly basis. I don't know about you, but I don't miss money that I never see. Hopefully, you won't either.

If you are working on a project, make sure that things are done right the first time, even if you have to pay extra money for quality. In other words, don't be cheap. Sometimes you end up wasting more time and money when you cut corners. I know this from firsthand experience. I was once working on a big project and in an effort to save money I hired a certain graphic designer simply because he offered to do the work at a low rate. Well as the saying goes, I got what I paid for. The designer lacked professionalism, and he did not meet the deadline we established. Plus the quality of the work was poor. In the end, my time and money was wasted and I had to pay a new designer even more money to get the job done. Don't make the same mistake. Pay for quality and peace of mind.

Be sure to put away your cash and save. Have at least six months of living expenses saved up just in case you lose your job or business slows down. I don't care if you start by saving five dollars a week. It's a start. After you develop momentum, saving will become easier. Also, have an emergency fund prepared just in case.

In the end I want you to have a system and be in the habit of saving money. I want you to be in the wealth preservation business and try to save as much money as you can. Wealth preservation is self-preservation. I hear people say, "What's the big deal? You can't take it with you when you die." My response to that is, "You must be planning to die soon because the people who save money have the means to take care of themselves in the later years of their life." A human's first instinct is to survive. Why deal with stress and high blood pressure over financial issues when we can prevent it by making smart choices?

You have the choice to do what is right for your life. It is all up to you. We are the results of the choices we made in the past. The difference between people who are successful in recovery and those that are not, are their choices. It will always be this way.

PERSONAL BUDGET

Many people become angry, depressed, or stressed out due to poor financial management. On this page, create a monthly budget for yourself based on your current income.

Mortgage/Rent: _____

Utilities: _____

Groceries: _____

Insurance: _____

Cell Phone: _____

Internet: _____

Credit Card: Entertainment/Self Care:

_____   _____

Clothing: Gas:

_____   _____

Misc.:   Savings:

_____   _____

Money in   -   **Money out**   =   **Money left**

Budget Notes:

_____

Notes:

_____

_____

_____

_____

_____

_____

_____

_____

DECISION MAKING SCENARIOS

Behavior is developed through our values, principles and the consequences of our actions. Each decision or choice that you make has a ripple effect. We would like for you to practice your decision making skills while being exposed to emotionally charged scenarios. There are no right or wrong answers. We just want you to practice making decisions while being emotionally charged.

If you want to get better at singing, public speaking, driving a car, painting, or doing some other skill, you need to practice. People who live the best lives make the best decisions. We want you to make the best decisions for your life.

On the next page, there is a series of scenarios for you to evaluate. Please have a response for each scenario listed. Please keep it real and don't give answers that you think your group or counselor want to hear. Remember this is a judgment free zone.

Scenario # 4

You're watching the news and you see video footage of a man that is wanted by the police for murdering a woman and burning her body on the side of the road near your house. The man looks exactly like your brother. Just a week before, on the night of the murder, your brother came to your house looking worried and asking for a gas can. Although you didn't give him your gas can, you noticed later on that it was missing. What would you do?

_____

_____

_____

_____

_____

_____

_____

_____

Scenario # 7

You are struggling financially and your neighbor is "getting over" because she is getting disability, food stamps, and a tax return for three kids that are not hers. Plus she has a babysitting business next door and is not licensed by the state to run a daycare.

1) Do you report her?

2) Do you blackmail her to get a cut of her money?

3) Do you ignore the situation and mind your business?

4) Other_____

Scenario # 8

You get laid off from work and receive your final check. With this check you now have a total of $800 left to your name to pay your $700 rent, $300 car note, and $200 in utility bills. It is your daughter's sixth birthday next week. How do you handle this situation? What will be your strategy?

_____

_____

_____

_____

_____

_____

_____

_____

Scenario # 9

You are hanging out at your friend's house watching football and he decides to invite more people over to watch the game. These are all of the people that you used to steal with before you entered treatment. How will you handle this situation?

_____

_____

_____

_____

_____

_____

_____

MINDSET MAINTENANCE

✓ Know your triggers and stay away from them.

✓ Find alternate ways to cope.

✓ Go to counseling for un-resolved issues like grief, depression, anger, anxiety, domestic violence, substance use, or a gambling or sex addiction.

✓ Engage in activities that improve your mood (manage your emotions).

✓ Do positive things that you used to enjoy that you don't do now (nostalgia, music, hobbies, old television shows).

✓ Try something new and gain exposure to exciting things that interest you.

✓ Resolve personal issues with family, friends and coworkers.

✓ Be assertive and do not be afraid to tell people "no."

✓ Be aware and adjust your behavior patterns.

✓ Stay away from negative influences.

✓ Develop an action plan to improve emotionally, physically, and financially.

✓ Understand the long-term consequences of your actions and how it will affect you personally, professionally, and emotionally.

✓ Practice delayed gratification.

✓ Create a budget for yourself and only buy what you need and save for the future.

✓ When you have the urge to engage in negative behaviors, know that you have a choice. You are not on auto-pilot and you can control your behavior.

✓ Go to school and improve your marketability by earning a degree, trade, or license in a specialized field. Work on professional goals.

✓ Exercise regularly and try to get sunlight as much as possible to increase endorphins.

✓ Do positive things and engage in legal experiences that make you happy.

✓ Develop a relapse prevention plan. Pre-plan on how you are going to respond to stress, anxiety, failure, and mistakes in a positive manner that lead to long-term success.

✓ Get spiritual guidance.

TIME MANAGEMENT

Goals   Priority   Deadline

1. _____   _____   _____

2. _____   _____   _____

3. _____   _____   _____

4. _____   _____   _____

5. _____   _____   _____

Time   Activity   Time   Activity

_____   _____   _____   _____

Monday

_____   _____   _____   _____

_____   _____   _____   _____

_____   _____   _____   _____

_____   _____   _____   _____

Time   Activity   Time   Activity

_____   _____   _____   _____

Tuesday

_____   _____   _____   _____

_____   _____   _____   _____

_____   _____   _____   _____

_____   _____   _____   _____

Time   Activity   Time   Activity

_____   _____   _____   _____

Wednesday

_____   _____   _____   _____

_____   _____   _____   _____

_____   _____   _____   _____

_____   _____   _____   _____

Time   Activity   Time   Activity

_____   _____   _____   _____

Thursday

_____   _____   _____   _____

_____   _____   _____   _____

_____   _____   _____   _____

_____   _____   _____   _____

Time   Activity   Time   Activity

_____   _____   _____   _____

Friday

_____   _____   _____   _____

_____   _____   _____   _____

_____   _____   _____   _____

_____   _____   _____   _____

Time   Activity   Time   Activity

_____   _____   _____   _____

Saturday

_____   _____   _____   _____

_____   _____   _____   _____

_____   _____   _____   _____

_____   _____   _____   _____

Time   Activity   Time   Activity

_____   _____   _____   _____

Sunday

_____   _____   _____   _____

_____   _____   _____   _____

_____   _____   _____   _____

_____   _____   _____   _____

Time   Activity   Time   Activity

_____   _____   _____   _____

SETTING GOALS

Write a list of short-term and long-term goals that you would like to accomplish.

_____

_____

_____

_____

Transform your list of goals into SMART goals by answering the following questions. Start with the first goal listed above.

Goal:

_____

_____

_____

_____

Specific: What specifically do you want to do?

_____

_____

_____

_____

Measurable: How will you measure your success? How much? How many?

_____

_____

_____

_____

Attainable: Is it in your power to accomplish this goal?

_____

_____

_____

_____

Relevant: Is this goal consistent with your other goals and plans.

_____

_____

_____

_____

Time-bound: What is the established deadline that will create a reasonable sense of urgency for you to complete the goal?

_____

_____

_____

_____

SMART Goal:

_____

_____

_____

_____

PROFESSIONAL DEVELOPMENT

What can you specialize in that makes you different from the crowd? What special skill, niche, or talent can you develop that will put you in demand?

Go on the internet and search for careers that require a special skill or training that you would be willing to commit to. Look for something that most people are not doing or thinking about. Look for apprenticeship and certification programs. Do not be discouraged if it requires you to jump through a lot of hoops. This element is created to weed out competition and the people who are not serious.

Sample Careers:

Food Stylist	Deep Sea Welder	Horse Exerciser
Trauma Cleanup	Polygraph Examiner	Millwright
Glass Blower	Cremator	Mediator
Elevator Inspector	Locomotive Engineer	Foley Artist

List the careers that you are interested in

_____

_____

Transferable Skills

Many who have committed acts of theft transfer their experience to work as consultants to prevent acts of check fraud, robbery, credit card fraud, shoplifting, theft, cheating, embezzlement, etc.

They work for:

- ✓ FBI
- ✓ Casinos
- ✓ Banking Industry
- ✓ Loss Prevention
- ✓ Treatment Programs
- ✓ Internet Security
- ✓ Law Enforcement
- ✓ Accounting Firms

Jobs to avoid in early recovery

- ✓ Baby Sitting
- ✓ Cleaning Services
- ✓ Jewelry Stores
- ✓ Grocery Stores
- ✓ Clothing Stores
- ✓ Retail Stores
- ✓ Installation
- ✓ Electronic Stores
- ✓ Plumbing
- ✓ Department Stores
- ✓ Liquor Stores

SELF-CARE

There are those in this world who fail to take care of themselves. Due to this, they suffer at work, have poor relationships, live shorter lives, use illegal drugs to cope, etc. It is important that we take care of ourselves. Check the things that you would like to do to improve your self-care.

_____Massages

_____Vacation

_____Manicures

_____Pedicures

_____Facials

_____Staycation

_____Alone time

_____Sunlight

_____Exercise

_____Be in Nature

_____Socialize

_____Counseling

_____Improve Living Environment

_____Improve Work Environment

_____Buy New Clothes

_____Sleep

_____Read

_____Improve Eating Habits

_____Hobbies

_____Other

BELIEVE IN YOURSELF

If you can control your emotions, you can control your life. But first, you have to believe in yourself.

Believability Scale

1_____2_____3_____4_____5_____6_____7_____8_____9_____10

On a scale of one to ten, one being the lowest and ten being the highest, circle the number that represents your belief that you will not steal again. If you circle ten, that means you are very confident. If you circle one, that means that you are not confident.

1. Explain why you chose the number you circled.

_____

_____

_____

_____

2. What can you do to increase your belief?

_____

_____

_____

_____

_____

_____

_____

_____

_____

_____

_____

_____

_____

_____

_____

ACCOUNTABILITY PARTNERS

Sometimes we need assistance in being accountable for our action or inaction. Accountability partners can help us stay on track with our goals by checking our progress. They tell us what we need to hear, not what we want to hear. Accountability partners tell us the truth and are not enablers. They are invested in our long-term success. They can be friends, family members, or co-workers.

Write down the qualities of a great accountability partner.

_____

_____

_____

_____

Do you feel it is important for someone to hold you accountable?

Yes or No

Write down names of potential accountability partners who you trust to hold you accountable. Be careful in who you choose. Everyone is not meant to be an accountability partner. The person you choose may have great qualities, but may not be great in holding people accountable.

Potential Accountability Partners	What qualities do they have?

GRATITUDE

We sometimes forget about our blessings and take them for granted. It is important to appreciate the things that we have. When you think about complaining always remember that things can be worse. Believe it or not, there are people in this world that wish they were in your position.

List the things that you are thankful for.

_____

_____

_____

_____

_____

_____

_____

People take care of the things that they truly appreciate. For example, if someone appreciates their car, they keep their car clean and make sure that they keep up on the maintenance. Appreciation is more than saying words. It is consists of feeling thankful and doing things that show that you are appreciative.

List the things that you can do to show your appreciation.

_____

_____

_____

_____

_____

_____

BUCKET LIST

Write down a list of things that you want to do before you die.

_____

_____

_____

_____

_____

_____

_____

_____

_____

_____

What steps do you need to take now to accomplish the things listed on your bucket list?

_____

_____

_____

_____

_____

_____

_____

_____

_____

_____

_____

EXAM

1. List five anger management strategies.

_____

_____

_____

_____

_____

2. List five strategies that can be used to overcome depression.

_____

_____

_____

_____

_____

3. List five strategies that you can use to prevent yourself from shoplifting.

_____

_____

_____

_____

_____

4. List all seven phases a person may go through when they are tempted to steal.

_____

_____

_____

_____

5. List five strategies that can help improve your self-esteem.

_____

_____

_____

6. What is your relapse prevention plan used for?

_____

_____

_____

_____

7. According to research, what are the top two reasons why the majority of people shoplift or steal?

_____

_____

_____

_____

8. List five cons of theft.

_____

_____

_____

_____

9. List all of the stages of change.

_____

_____

_____

_____

10. Define emotional intelligence.

_____

_____

_____

_____

THEFT AND SHOPLIFTING LOG

Week 1

Rank your desire to steal or shoplift on scale from one to ten. One being lowest and ten being highest.

1   2   3   4   5   6   7   8   9   10

Please explain your ranking for this week

_____

_____

_____

_____

Week 2

Rank your desire to steal or shoplift on scale from one to ten. One being lowest and ten being highest.

1   2   3   4   5   6   7   8   9   10

Please explain your ranking for this week

_____

_____

_____

_____

Week 3

Rank your desire to steal or shoplift on scale from one to ten. One being lowest and ten being highest.

1   2   3   4   5   6   7   8   9   10

Please explain your ranking for this week

_____

_____

_____

_____

Week 4

Rank your desire to steal or shoplift on scale from one to ten. One being lowest and ten being highest.

1   2   3   4   5   6   7   8   9   10

Please explain your ranking for this week

_____

_____

_____

_____

Week 5

Rank your desire to steal or shoplift on scale from one to ten. One being lowest and ten being highest.

1   2   3   4   5   6   7   8   9   10

Please explain your ranking for this week

_____

_____

_____

_____

Week 6

Rank your desire to steal or shoplift on scale from one to ten. One being lowest and ten being highest.

1   2   3   4   5   6   7   8   9   10

Please explain your ranking for this week

_____

_____

_____

_____

Week 7

Rank your desire to steal or shoplift on scale from one to ten. One being lowest and ten being highest.

1   2   3   4   5   6   7   8   9   10

Please explain your ranking for this week

_____

_____

_____

_____

Week 8

Rank your desire to steal or shoplift on scale from one to ten. One being lowest and ten being highest.

1   2   3   4   5   6   7   8   9   10

Please explain your ranking for this week

_____

_____

_____

Week 9

Rank your desire to steal or shoplift on scale from one to ten. One being lowest and ten being highest.

1   2   3   4   5   6   7   8   9   10

Please explain your ranking for this week

_____

_____

_____

Week 10

Rank your desire to steal or shoplift on scale from one to ten. One being lowest and ten being highest.

1   2   3   4   5   6   7   8   9   10

Please explain your ranking for this week

_____

_____

_____

Week 11

Rank your desire to steal or shoplift on scale from one to ten. One being lowest and ten being highest.

1   2   3   4   5   6   7   8   9   10

Please explain your ranking for this week

_____

_____

Week 12

Rank your desire to steal or shoplift on scale from one to ten. One being lowest and ten being highest.

1   2   3   4   5   6   7   8   9   10

Please explain your ranking for this week

_____

_____

_____

Week 13

Rank your desire to steal or shoplift on scale from one to ten. One being lowest and ten being highest.

1   2   3   4   5   6   7   8   9   10

Please explain your ranking for this week

_____

_____

_____

Week 14

Rank your desire to steal or shoplift on scale from one to ten. One being lowest and ten being highest.

1   2   3   4   5   6   7   8   9   10

Please explain your ranking for this week

_____

_____

_____

Week 15

Rank your desire to steal or shoplift on scale from one to ten. One being lowest and ten being highest.

1   2   3   4   5   6   7   8   9   10

Please explain your ranking for this week

_____

_____

Week 16

Rank your desire to steal or shoplift on scale from one to ten. One being lowest and ten being highest.

1   2   3   4   5   6   7   8   9   10

Please explain your ranking for this week

_____

_____

_____

Week 17

Rank your desire to steal or shoplift on scale from one to ten. One being lowest and ten being highest.

1   2   3   4   5   6   7   8   9   10

Please explain your ranking for this week

_____

_____

_____

Week 18

Rank your desire to steal or shoplift on scale from one to ten. One being lowest and ten being highest.

1   2   3   4   5   6   7   8   9   10

Please explain your ranking for this week

_____

_____

_____

Week 19

Rank your desire to steal or shoplift on scale from one to ten. One being lowest and ten being highest.

1   2   3   4   5   6   7   8   9   10

Please explain your ranking for this week

_____

_____

Week 20

Rank your desire to steal or shoplift on scale from one to ten. One being lowest and ten being highest.

1   2   3   4   5   6   7   8   9   10

Please explain your ranking for this week

_____

_____

_____

_____

Week 21

Rank your desire to steal or shoplift on scale from one to ten. One being lowest and ten being highest.

1   2   3   4   5   6   7   8   9   10

Please explain your ranking for this week

_____

_____

_____

_____

Week 22

Rank your desire to steal or shoplift on scale from one to ten. One being lowest and ten being highest.

1   2   3   4   5   6   7   8   9   10

Please explain your ranking for this week

_____

_____

_____

_____

Week 23

Rank your desire to steal or shoplift on scale from one to ten. One being lowest and ten being highest.

1   2   3   4   5   6   7   8   9   10

Please explain your ranking for this week

_____

_____

Week 24

Rank your desire to steal or shoplift on scale from one to ten. One being lowest and ten being highest.

1   2   3   4   5   6   7   8   9   10

Please explain your ranking for this week